A Gay-Straight Christian Dialogue

A Little More Conversation, A Little Less Reaction, Please

'Michael' and 'Chris'

Anglican Parish Clergy In The North Of England

GW00808736

GROVE BOOKS LIMITED
RIDLEY HALL RD   CAMBRIDGE   CB3 9HU

Contents

First Impression December 2005
ISSN 0144-171X
ISBN 1 85174 609 9

Introduction

This booklet is an exercise in listening.

In committing itself to listen to the experiences of gay people within the church, the Anglican Communion set about a task which cannot be achieved through debate or argument. Too often debate involves waiting for the other party to speak while at the same time preparing one's own riposte. Voices are heard, but not received; arguments rehearsed but the people behind them left unacknowledged.

Dialogue, or conversation, will take us to different places. In this conversation, over a virtual pot of tea which represents a great deal of tea-drinking, discussion and friendship over a number of years, Michael and Chris explore together what it means to be friends. And one intrinsic part of that friendship is Chris's identity as a gay Christian minister.

Conversation is not the place to find tightly-argued analysis or detailed biblical exegesis. What it does provide is a meeting point between two human beings, and in this case two human beings who see that conversation as an opportunity to explore their identity and experience as Christian people in God's church. Chris's experience as a gay Christian needs to be heard, to be pondered, and maybe this is a book best read with a pot of tea and with time not to rush through. As Chris says, you know more gay people than you think you know, and listening to his experience may open the way to listening better to other people around us too.

'Michael' and 'Chris' are pseudonyms. The church of God is not (yet) the place of grace, of safe space, which it needs to be if some gay Christians are to come out of the closet without fear. In letting us in on their conversation, Michael and Chris allow us the chance to see how that grace, that safety, might be expressed. My hope is that this open conversation will lead to the start of other similar expressions of dialogue across the church, to a little more conversation and a little less reaction.

Mike Booker

Grove Pastoral Group

2

You and Me Song

Call me Michael. It's not my real name, but here I am, a vicar sitting at my desk somewhere in the north of England looking out over a field with a farm and trees in the distance. It's many shades of green and it's rural! It's a little while after my 30th birthday and I'm committed to Christ.

In that case, call me Chris. It's not my real name, either, but it'll do for now. And I'm a vicar on the other side of the Pennines, a little while longer after my 30th birthday. By the grace of God, I'm trying to help grow the kingdom on the streets of a big city.

We met at theological college when we were in our twenties. My childhood background witnessed some contact with the Christian faith, as my family had connections with the local parish church. I hated the occasions when I was made to go to church by my parents—it was so boring and dull. However, I loved going to midnight mass, if only for the joy of staying up late at Christmas and poking fun at the vicar's receding hairline. I had to leave home and go to university in order to encounter God moving in mysterious ways within my life. University was a place of personal discovery; of conversations late into the night on all sorts of topics and issues; of debates and discussions with the chaplain and other Christians, with a healthy dose of prayer and Bible reading thrown in. So, after three years there faith in Christ had taken root and was beginning to grow. The next step in my journey was to be a church youth worker, exploring a call to the ordained ministry of the Church of England. And then a theological college somewhere in England welcomed me through its doors. And whom did I meet there?

I take it you mean me. I grew up in a Midlands comprehensive under the Conservative government and I had no church background beyond my infant baptism. Then—full of angst and in my late teens—I was persuaded to attend a carol service one desultory Christmas. Suddenly, all the stories of Jesus from my religious studies GCSE made sense, as if my flawed grasp of the gospels had been given a good shake. I gave my life to Christ on the spot, and he spent my three years at university giving me a grounding in the faith. Then he led me to take two years out working in churches of wildly different descriptions before the Church of England decided I should train to be ordained. And from there it all looked remarkably straightforward—not easy, but at least straightforward. Get trained, find a curacy and my part in ministering to God's world…It's never that straightforward, is it?

For me many things at college were straightforward, which may have something to do with being fairly laid back. However, there were challenges: adjusting to being in a new place, embarking on a new process with new people and — above all — freshly married. But God was good and provided a safe place to live and a number of good people with whom to train.

Three years of theological education wasn't too traumatic. But three years of godly formation…God had me just where he wanted me, to work on me as a human being and to do all the preparation work that I'd neglected during my busy gap years. I'd been intermittently quite depressed in the previous months but not really had the awareness, the courage or the support to address it. I recall one terrible Boxing Day when I was alone and in total desperation in Yorkshire and it felt like my head was about to explode under the pressure of despair. But at theological college God provided the time—and at least some of the people—to start facing up to a few facts. There were a number of things to face, but the biggest emerged over one summer. I was not—and am not—attracted to women, no matter how hard I tried. The whole of my sexual attraction has been—and is—towards men. You could bring in a dozen of the most sexually desirable women in history—Kylie, Jordan, Felicity Kendal, whoever—and sexually I wouldn't feel a thing for any of them (although Felicity's autograph would be nice). You could bring in a dozen of the male equivalents—Orlando Bloom, Josh Hartnett, James McAvoy—and result! That would float my boat, turn a light on in my corner, stir my loins. So you can see I finally had to concede to myself that I was gay. Bent as a nine bob note. Queer as dick's hatband. Homo faggot poof, as people used to say at school. And being broadly evangelical, having grown up in a time before EastEnders and having a vocation to work for God…well, it was less than straightforward.

3

A Red Letter Day

It's fun having a typeface all to myself. The only drawback is that people have to imagine our tones of voice. So let me clear that one up now. I could be angry. This could be some sort of polemic. I could be self-pitying or grinding an axe. Anything. There aren't any stage directions either. I could be sitting slumped with my head in my hands. Or kicking in chairs and knocking down tables. Or standing proud in pink lycra and waving a flag. As it happens, I'm not. Neither of us are. We're sitting on a sofa drinking tea and eating toast.

That's the best way to imagine this conversation. Two friends trying to get at some truth, two friends listening and talking, talking and listening.

And I'm only talking for me. I'm the only person I can speak for. You extrapolate from me to other gay, lesbian or bisexual people at your own risk. But I trust that some of what I say comes close to what we might hear from anyone who is angry or self-pitying, head in hands or loud and proud in pink spandex. None of which are mutually exclusive. And most of which could be me in some other mood at some other time of day. Except for the spandex. Anyway, back to the story.

So it was that after two years of being friends and two years into training…

…two years of sharing dreams about the church and our ministry…

…and two years of drinking tea, eating toast and listening to a plethora of 80's and 90's electronic music that it came down to a Friday morning when, with a lecture cancelled, you said you needed to talk.

I think I exhausted my adrenalin supplies just saying that much.

You told me you were gay.

I did, but not quite so directly! I'd been living in a faintly evangelical theological college for more than two years and I was more than anything afraid of the consequences to my life, my ministry and my mental health if word got out that I was gay. On top of that I was still wrestling with all the voices from the past, the Midlands and the church that being gay was a deeply shameful thing. I'd concluded that what I needed was a wider circle of people—to create some safe company in which to work out all the complications—social and theological—of it all. Now you were a prime candidate, and I'd decided to talk to you, but I was still absolutely bricking myself at the prospect. This cancelled lecture had all the hallmarks of an opportunity from God. So I took a deep breath, made a pot of tea, beat around the bush for a quarter of an hour and told you.

> Now, at the time of being told, it didn't hit me like a bombshell. I kind of knew it or, if I didn't, it made sense to me. On the other hand, it would take some thinking through—and what were the consequences for me? We were friends with much in common, but this was the first time I had found myself being told by a friend that he was gay. In many ways I found this was quite a scary position to be in. What should I say or not say? Had I said or done anything in the past which was offensive and hurtful? But we were friends and to my mind this was neither the time nor the issue for that friendship to be put in jeopardy. You'd put yourself, Chris, in a very vulnerable and trusting position, which I had to respect. I don't remember much of the conversation, do you?

I remember the strangest things about it. I recall that once I'd said I needed to talk to you, I'd more or less created a sense of gravity which could only be warranted by one of two things: being gay or being terminally ill. How surreal is that? Why should an accidental sexual preference come anywhere near something as serious as life-threatening illness? I was very thankful that a pot of tea (or three) was involved in the conversation, because I desperately needed something to cling onto, and a mug of tea fitted the bill. Am I getting across just how scary and uncertain and momentous this occasion was?

> Yes you are. I agree with you—how strange that sexual preference and life-threatening illnesses should be perceived as equally grave.

The other very strange thing I experienced was the compulsion to let you know that there was no question of me fancying you—perhaps not the greatest compliment in the world. Anything to say about that?

> **Well, I can't have it all and the feeling is mutual! On a more serious level, though, I believe I felt a certain sense of relief, and, of course, by saying this you immediately answered a question that would have entered my mind at some point. Also, it reflects just how open you felt you could be in talking to me—and highlights the risk you were personally taking in talking to me.**

It's fascinating what you said a moment ago about putting friendships in jeopardy. I'd been afraid that something I said might mean you breaking off our friendship. It hadn't really occurred to me that the circumstances—that my revelation—had put you under a similar pressure, put you in a position where you were afraid that something you might say might lead to the end of our friendship, broken off by me...

> **Yes, in the light of your revelation the foundations of our friendship from my side needed some internal reflection and because of that caused some uncertainty. Perhaps it was along the lines that, 'if Chris has been this honest with me about himself, how honest could he be about what he thinks of me, and if so what might he say that could jeopardise our friendship.' This seems illogical now I'm saying it, but there we are.**

And then we went for a long walk, which was a very good idea. I find talking face-to-face about my sexuality very difficult, even with a friend. Even now, if we ever talk about sexuality I prefer to be driving somewhere, both of us looking in the same forwards direction and not at each other. It felt—and it still feels—a very intimate and personal thing to talk about, and I'm by no means the most outgoing of people.

> **I feel the same really—it's easier to talk whilst doing something else, like walking or driving. Anyway, being a Friday, the weekend gave me the opportunity to consider what you'd told me about yourself.**

So we went our separate ways for the weekend. I was pretty relieved—not to mention wiped out by the effort! Even with a good friend, telling someone that I'm gay is a lot like giving someone a knife and wondering if they'll stab me in the back with it. On top of everything, was I about to lose someone with whom I'd shared so much in the preceding two years? But when Monday came, you were still you. I'd been irrationally afraid that you might not broach the whole gay subject again. And that would have been as effective a rejection as anything. But we're getting ahead of ourselves. There's a lot to colour in and clarify between admitting to myself that I was gay and admitting it to you.

4   Life of Surprises

Well. You remember how much I had to beat around the bush before I actually said to you, 'Michael, I think I'm gay'? Well, that's nothing compared to the length of time it took me to admit it to myself. If I'm honest I was well into my early 20s before I was able to talk to myself about it. It's quite hard to express just how unthinkable it was for me to be gay—or rather, just how difficult it would have been to survive healthily in my own head in the Midlands as a teenager—or later, in a thriving evangelical church—if I'd been that honest with myself. So to cut a long story short, I managed to keep the truth from myself for a long time. Part of me knew, but part of me was kept very much in the dark. We'll have a look at that; but first, tell me—as you grew up, what gay people were you aware of and what did you think of them?

> **The first thing that comes to mind is watching** *Top of the Pops* **and seeing Boy George and Culture Club and Holly Johnson and Frankie Goes to Hollywood in the mid 80s. And at the same time the AIDS scare and hard-hitting adverts warning about the risks of unprotected sex. Gay people weren't part of normal life—they were on TV, dressing extravagantly, being pop stars, and even threatening normal life—they were seen as responsible for spreading AIDS.**
>
> **In hindsight, this seems crazy; and of course, as I became more informed about HIV/AIDS I dropped this prejudice against gay people. I never knew anyone who was openly gay at school; it would have been virtually impossible for anyone to come out. They would have been ridiculed.**

Ridiculed or slaughtered! Taken to pieces every day and left out to dry, I imagine. Boys aren't slow to make 'backs to the wall' bummer jokes. As I grew up there was Larry Grayson on *The Generation Game* and John Inman on *Are You Being Served?* And there were the Village People (although in retrospect not many of them were actually gay). Gay people were seen as flamboyant, effete, limp-wristed. Nowadays there's a much wider and more balanced cast of gay characters both in public life and on the television—

Grange Hill, Byker Grove, Coronation Street. So there is mileage being made in terms of showing that gay people are pretty ordinary, but I'm not sure how far that idea permeates into society or schools. Anyway, from at least the age of eight I was very much aware of feelings of same-sex attraction. I'd be watching television and find myself totally confused, totally overwhelmed by a feeling, and there was nobody to whom I could talk about it. I fancied quite a few men off *Top of the Pops*, a character or two in science fiction drama, and one of the leads of Press Gang—among many others! And while my peers were exploring heterosexual relationships and seeing how far they could go, I was keeping it all in my head—even keeping it from my own conscious self.

It must have been a lonely time. You're right in saying that gay people are now increasingly shown as pretty ordinary folk by TV and radio drama, but it appears to me that this can be part of the problem—gay people are just a part of fictional drama—'on TV and radio is fine but not within my family and friends.' What do you think?

You're absolutely right about the loneliness. There was an important hungry part of me that I was never able to talk about or even begin to make sense of. Fortunately people like the Pet Shop Boys were out there making music—good, literate, lyrical music—that made me suspect that there were people out there who understood a little. But that was a very slender comfort. Time went by, puberty set in, and suddenly the nights and my dreams were just as dangerous as daylight and television! I imagine it's bad enough trying to smuggle your stiffening sheets through the washing machine without the added weight of knowing you were dreaming about your own gender! Then I got away to university and I was actually rubbing shoulders with attractive people. With hindsight there were a few moments of great potential there, where almost anything could have happened...but they were always thwarted by this whole gay thing being unthinkable, in my head at least. There was an ever-present backdrop of disapproval from much of the world, a background radiation of shame that meant I was increasingly living in fear, guilt and denial for over 15 years. And that's bad for self-esteem, bad for mental health, bad for most things. That's one of the things I think I'll like most about the new heaven and the new earth—all that white noise of disapproval in print and on television and from some people will fade to silence!

What strikes me most about hearing you say this is how similar my thoughts and experiences were. The sheets, the attractive women, the freedom of being away from home and the watchful eyes of my parents. Unfortunately, it wasn't so unthinkable, and I had to learn the hard way of the damaging emotional effects of sex without love and commitment. However, I did have Christian friends who were there for me, who listened, loved, cared and forgave. I was given safe space to share my feelings, pain and disappointments; and God filled that safe space with his presence and healing. Now, it seems to me that my safe space had more of a social and Christian validity because I'm straight. You undoubtedly wish to have a safe space this side of the new heaven and new earth.

That's exactly it. Being gay is just like being straight in most respects. The attraction, the embarrassment, the stiffies. That sort of space you describe is just the sort of space I didn't have. In theological college, the cumulative noise made by my sexuality inside my head finally grew strong enough to tear through the increasingly thin veil that was keeping me from admitting it to myself. It was assisted by the onset of a serious depression, which laid me low for a long time. Suddenly everything came together and I had to say, 'Right. I'm gay, I'm training to be a vicar and I'm surrounded by Christians. Oh pants.' Christians are rather double-edged! It's hard to forget news reports of Christians waving placards about fags and queers. The saints do some funny things. As I said, talking to anybody is like offering them a knife and waiting to see whether they plunge it hilt-deep in my back or simply cut a slice of lemon Madeira and put the kettle on. Fortunately, God had provided quite a cast of kind and loving and patient people, the sort who'd not stick the knife in. But as you may recall, it still took me a long time to decide to trust you with something this serious, and then weeks to pluck up the courage to do it.

Yeah, trust. You had to decide to trust me, and it took a long time. I had it with my friends at university, but just how did you come to decide that I was someone you could trust?

I don't know. How does anyone decide whom they trust? A huge part of it was simply the weight of support and good humour I'd seen in you, not least through my depression. It was your capacity to forgive, and to stick with me when I was probably quite a burden and not too full of sunshine, and when it was probably unclear what you could do to help someone laid so low. It was the prayers and the sense of humour. And of course it was much more than that—something indescribable that the Bible touches on when it talks about a friend who sticks closer than a brother.

However, you could have been all of those things and somehow not made the grade. In the days between admitting to myself that I was gay and talking to people, there was a subconscious process of auditioning going on—listening to people. At that time I could have drawn up a league table of people, both in theological college and beyond, who'd said either positive or negative things about gayness. When I was living with fear, a negative comment weighed very heavily but a positive one was treated very cautiously. Even now, I know who's spoken about the subject in my hearing and how positively they've portrayed themselves as someone who might be a source of support and a good friend. That's a natural survival instinct and it's not limited to matters of sexuality or to gay people. People across my parishes, knowingly or not, are making prospective judgments about whether or not they would find a good friend and a source of support in me with a problem they might have. It brings a whole new layer of meaning to the 'cloud of unseen witnesses' around us.

And let me tell you something fascinating. It's hardly about doctrine at all. I've trusted in people with all shades of opinion about the Bible and about sexuality. The key has been—is this person a kind person? I'm not, in the first instance, looking for people to help me out with what I think about being gay. I can hear the arguments everywhere—there's not much chance of missing them! I look for people who listen a lot and talk a little less, who aren't particularly shocked by things...kind people.

I agree with you completely about kindness—it reminds me of the fruit of the Spirit. Kind people are open and attractive; they invite trust. All my friends at university were, and still are, kind people at heart. And I believe our friendship has kindness right down there in its foundations. So, slightly tongue in cheek, do you think that kind people know more gay people?

Most people know someone who's gay, I'm sure. Kind people don't just know gay people, they get to know that those people are gay. If you see what I mean? I still have friends, colleagues and acquaintances who seem to think I'm straight. Like you said earlier, there are people with different views of the world. There are people who know there are gay men and women in the world, but somehow assume that they're all 'out there' somewhere—on television or the Archers, in London or Manchester but not in their street, their workplace, their family or their church. Gay people are perhaps more visible on television or in Manchester, but gay people aren't limited to big cities, boy bands and variety shows. It's sad, because someone might say something about the 'queers' who are 'out there' and not realize that I'm not out there, I'm in here with them! It happened to me twice last week and I was gutted—both for me and for the people talking so carelessly. Maybe the thing to learn is this: tread lightly and speak carefully, because you know more gay people than you think you know. And not just gay people, but people with secret traumas of all kinds.

> **Treading lightly and speaking carefully is good, whatever subject we are talking about, not just homosexuality. I know we all say things we regret from time to time, but regarding homosexuality I very often hear people speaking carelessly, and with very little discernment. Perhaps they haven't got the vocabulary to express what they mean, or they just really are prejudiced. But it's sad to meet Christians whose language and attitude lack charity and kindness towards gay people. Would I be jumping the gun in thinking that the two careless people last week were both Christians?**

You'd be right. That's the tragic part; I've heard it said that Christians are the only army who shoot their own wounded. I try not to hold a grudge, but that sort of thing does cast a long sad shadow over our future dealings.

And just as Christians are a double-edged phenomenon, so are family. A great deal of well-being, happiness and security—or on the other hand isolation, misery and practical disadvantages —depend on just how someone's family respond to the news—if indeed one feels inclined to tell them! My parents are pretty damn good, although I wasn't sure about that until after I'd broken the news. I don't know the statistics about the proportion of under-standing family members but there are certainly some gay people for whom family rejection is a major possibility and a particularly horrible extra difficulty.

> **It seems another huge weight to carry around and risk to take. Family relationships can be hard at the best of times, but to live with**

the fear of parental and family rejection on top of the existing social pressures must be very challenging. Communication within a family must play a big role. If members of a family can talk together on a deeper level than the state of the weather and the England football team, and with an attitude of love and kindness, there must be a better chance of that family being more understanding of each other's joys and difficulties in life.

Mind you, if you start talking about sexuality—and why shouldn't people?—you can feel like you're in a minefield. Would you like to take a stroll through it together?

5 Stereotypes

The sexuality minefield! Okay, so let's begin with what I said earlier. When I was younger most gay people seemed to me to be extravagant dressed pop stars who had lots of sex and spread AIDS. Ludicrously sad, narrow and misguided, and obviously I don't hold to that understanding now. But it seems to me that for a good many people this constitutes their entire understanding of gay people. So what, then, does the average person mean when they use terms such as gay, lesbian, and homosexual? Sadly, I think they are referring to sex, and probably lots of it—being gay equals gay sex. Having sex seems to dominate the whole gay agenda whether in church circles or society at large. I suppose it sells newspapers. What do you think?

Well, I'm not getting any! A wise man once told a joke: 'What do gay couples do in bed?'

I don't know. What *do* gay couples do in bed?

They drink Ovaltine and read books like everyone else. I don't know the figures but I think I can guarantee it's not all sex sex sex, just as much as being straight isn't all sex sex sex. Is it? Actually, what is being straight all about?

I thought you could tell me! Well, for one thing it's not all sex, sex, sex—although it's certainly got its place! Being straight is more about that simple word—living. Paying the bills, going to work, having a curry, watching the football, going to the cinema, being on the village hall committee, worshipping Jesus. I imagine it's pretty much the same for gay people. I have to say I don't drink Ovaltine in bed, but a good read—that's not bad!

Thankfully, nobody has ever asked me, 'What's being gay like?' You might as well ask, 'What's being straight like?' And I'd like to apologise here for any terrible stereotypes that gay people impose on straight people. You are not all aesthetically challenged, bad dancers with no style and bad hair. In fact that sounds suspiciously like me.

But I digress. What are the pervasive myths about being gay?

> Well I've already mentioned one—sex. Gay people are always having sex, right? And because they are having lots of sex, which isn't natural (for two reasons—because it's gay sex and because there's lots of it!), it must mean that gay people are also paedophiles. Basically, they like having lots of sex with each other and they like having sex with children.
>
> It's a disturbing link.

It's a combination of society scapegoating and the media scaremongering. Child sexual abuse is a horrible thing, and it's an easy road to save us believing that terrible things including paedophilia take place within families. If we must live in a world with awful things happening, it's reassuring to lay the blame somewhere else—and of course gay people are already seen as 'out there.' There's no link between these two things. It's such a red herring—and a damaging one for our children, because as long as we're looking 'out there' for culprits, we're missing the people 'in here' who are actually involved in child abuse.

But that spurious link and the nebulous fear surrounding it are quite toxic. I remember the first time I talked to our mutual friends Thomas and Anne about being gay. They have three children, and at the back of my head was this nauseous worry that they—sensible people though they are—might make that link and throw me out of their house, never ask me to babysit again...Of course they rose fantastically to the occasion—they're magnificent Christians. In retrospect it was stupid to think that they might harbour any ideas like that. But it takes a lot to dislodge that fear, and all the time that fear does nothing for my shaky nerves.

Here in the big city I wonder if my fear is more well-founded. If the parents at the schools where I take assemblies knew, perhaps understanding would be less forthcoming. The parallel concern that I might turn their children gay might arise...as if that's how people become gay! I've mixed with straight people all my life and haven't contracted heterosexuality yet. Or maybe your alchemy is simply on the blink?

> I agree, it's a crazy link really, and it leads you to a paralysing fear. It's as though people are thinking, 'One day they're "normal" and the next they're gay.' And I can almost hear people saying, 'For heaven's

sake, why be gay? Pull yourself together.' As with homosexuality and paedophilia, the logical consequence of people thinking it's a choice is that if someone chooses to be gay they must be perverted in some way—there must be something wrong with them.

Ah yes. Is it a perverse choice? Is it nature? Is it nurture? Is it genetic? Is it all down to a style of parenting or attributable to an over-emphasis of something in childhood years? Would you like the 100% cast-iron answer?

Please.

I don't know it. If we're honest, no-one knows it. Except God, and he's not telling. I'll tell you for nothing that when I was very small I was very attached to a pink teddy bear imaginatively called Pink Teddy. I'll tell you for nothing that I was last to arrive at primary school because of a staggered system of entry, and the only coat-hook left for me was one with a picture of a ballerina. But if you try to construct a grand unified theory of sexuality out of those things, I'll laugh a lot.

The whole question of cause seems to assume that all homosexuality is part of one monolithic, homogeneous mass. I can't see why anyone would assume that. But I'll tell you one thing: whether there's a gay gene, a gay upbringing or a mixture of the two, it's not a choice. I haven't consciously chosen to be gay. Having sexual relations or not—that's a choice; but being attracted to people of the same sex simply isn't. Why would I choose to be gay and face all the nerve-wracking things we've spoken about? Why choose to face the disapproval, the misunderstanding? I'm sure that there are circles in which sexual experimentation is much more accept-able, and I can even imagine people who affect a gay orientation to be fashionable, but those are rarefied circles indeed.

Then there are the stereotypes. As you've mentioned earlier, there's your limp-wristed, effeminate, high-pitched John Inman, your wild iconic pop star, and, perhaps in the minds of some, your monk or Roman Catholic priest. If someone expresses an 'unhealthy' interest in interior decorating or anything vaguely artistic or musical then they're also probably gay.

Do I fit any of those stereotypes?

Of course not, although you've put some pretty bold colours on the walls of your house, and I know that there are some stunning shirts in your wardrobe!

I don't wear tight spangly shirts (well, not often). I don't go mad for Cher. I've never watched a Barbra Streisand film, never seen *The Wizard of Oz* all the way through. I'm neither Tom out of *Gimme Gimme Gimme* nor Jack out of *Will and Grace*. There's a wonderful film called *In And Out* in which Kevin Kline sends up stereotypes beautifully—I think I made you watch it once. Go and watch it again.

Yes, it's a good film. One thing that comes to mind about Kevin Kline's character is that he had so much going on in his life. Being gay was not the be all and end all of his life.

I think what I'm driving at is that being gay is not my first, my last, my everything. It's not my most important characteristic. Long before I think of myself as gay, I think of myself as a Christian with all that it entails. Being gay is a little way down the list of what makes me the man I am, and it would be further down still if I could finally get my head round it. I cycle a lot, I write some odd poems, I love cinema and friends, and those things ought to tell you a lot more about me than some accident of sexuality over which I had no control.

Equally, however, it's not nothing. Being gay affects everything somehow, like a strand of my make-up that touches every other strand. Besides which, it affects my real life; the fact that I'm not married is just the most obvious! On a positive note, it might be true that my experiences as a gay man have made me a little more sympathetic to people who suffer or are seen as outsiders, or that I am slower to speak and take more care of people's hearts. On a sad note, I'm fairly sure that my life experiences as gay have made me more protective, more reserved, more abrasive. I'm not keen on those characteristics.

So being gay is not your all and everything, but it does affect all aspects of who you are. And I'd like to link this with what you said about being gay not being your choice, but that it is your choice whether to have sexual relations or not. Having taken a stroll through the sexuality minefield this seems to be one key issue; in what things do we or don't we have a choice?

Well, seven years since that first Friday, I'm still gay. I think that's worth saying. God is good and God can do anything, but my being gay is one thing he's not changed in these past half-dozen years. Occasionally I've entertained the notion that there might be a programme, a series of prayers, some process that would automatically and miraculously turn me around. But while God has the power and the prerogative, the kind of insistence that change is simply there for the asking seems to me misguided. I understand the desire to want to believe in that, but it does God an injustice. And I understand other people's desires to believe in that for me, to recommend or prescribe it—charitably because it might make my life easier, less charitably because it renders both God and the world much more cut and dried. I have a measure of faith in God, but nowhere do I find a promise that God *will* change my sexuality. He *can*. He *might*. However...my sober expectation, without closing any doors in the face of God, is that I will be gay for the rest of my life. But I'm ready to be surprised!

Anyway. We've talked about that Friday. We've talked about growing up. Let's talk about now.

This Is How It Feels

6

And let's pick up where we left off. This whole thing about me being gay isn't likely to blow over. I'm nine years older than when we met, possibly even a few weeks wiser. I'm ordained, my CD collection has grown, and I'm still gay. How about you?

I am also nine years older, I'm a father of two children, I'm ordained, I'm still straight, and we're still friends. One reason I believe our friendship has survived these years is the number of common interests we have—not least being ordained and having a collection of fantastic music. I know its survival is not because I've been holding onto the thought that one day you will be straight, will get married, have kids and we can all go off as families to Centre Parcs. I can't deny that I haven't thought about you changing from being gay to being straight, and wondering if and how God will do it, but then I've also wondered what it would be like if and how God changed my limited ability to kick a football like David Beckham. So, although I've had these thoughts from time to time, they don't enter the equation of what determines and upholds our friendship. I don't believe that God has encouraged our friendship for the purpose of me helping you change. I haven't done a very good job if he has!

Seven years ago—that Friday—when I was depressed and isolated, my biggest need was for space, for good people to help me through a very difficult and frightening time. That need has changed subtly. Nowadays I'm pretty cheerful, even if slightly reserved, and my needs in coping with this whole gay thing are less all-pervading. There's still the tinnitus, the background noise of prejudice and slighting comments, even if they're not aimed directly at me. But the moments of feeling simply very down about being gay are more isolated. The actual times at which you have to do or say something specific are intermittent, but the context of support and mutual friendship in which these are set is a lifelong context. So we each have to work on maintaining the kind of friendship in which we can help each other, and we each have to rise to the occasion when immediate and solid support is needed.

Make sense?

> Spot on. The support we give each other is nothing out of the ordinary. In many respects it's quite uneventful, very everyday and matter-of-fact. We meet when we can, we phone, we e-mail and sometimes send postcards from our holidays. Basic communication really. I think it's also important to say that the friendship and support is mutual. It's not about me, the straight one, befriending and supporting you, the gay one. Rather, we support each other at those times when support is needed, whatever the issue or reason. And we also have a laugh with each other at the funny things that come into our lives. Yes we've grown as individuals over these last seven years, but we're still very much who we were on that Friday. I don't know what the next seven years will bring our way, but our friendship has a good foundation upon which to trust each other in facing the ups and downs of the future.

Absolutely. Being a friend to anyone who's gay isn't hard. In fact, it's quite hard to get it wrong, but there are pitfalls. One or two of the people I've spoken to about it jumped straight to making sure that I wasn't sleeping with anybody—which might tell us something about where I featured in their priorities. One assumed I was sleeping with somebody and had drafted a letter to my rector and to the bishop before I knew it, accusing us of terrible things. One or two people have meant well and prescribed prayer to change me, and I felt like I was just some sort of problem to be diagnosed and ironed out—as if they couldn't handle the prospect of a Christian needing help with something over a lifetime. They wanted a quick fix for me, but I'm a bit of a fly in that particular ointment. Someone else seemed to decide I was the perfect figurehead for a crusade of her own views. But you, Michael, you listened to what I was saying. You didn't have an agenda for 'dealing with' gay people. There are people who've hastened to remind me what they say the Bible says—but I can reassure you that I've heard it a number of times! I'm just a person, but I am a person. I do get hurt. I have a heart and it bruises and bleeds and cries just like any other heart. I think that's worth remembering.

> Something that's different for us as we live out our lives is the time we spend in our homes. I have a wife and two young kids. We share the hard work and the relaxing moments, and we quite easily fill a house of four bedrooms and two bathrooms. Usually there will always

be someone around and something to do, so I rarely feel a sense of loneliness or uselessness. By contrast, Chris, you live alone in a fairly large house. Does that house feel like home to you?

Somewhere in Genesis God remarks that 'it's not good for man to be alone,' and he's not wrong! I work with people most of the time, and being alone can be refreshing, but equally there's nobody at hand when I arrive home to an empty house. This past week I've visited friends and everything takes a lot less effort when other people are around. In contrast when I'm alone there's a capacity for my heart to sink and sink. I have lots of good friends, although being a vicar means they're often around the country rather than around the corner, let alone around the house. So, yes, loneliness and isolation can be an issue. And equally, it's hard sometimes to find the motivation to do things or to make the house pleasant. Everything can feel a bit hollow unless it's shared with people. Read Armistead Maupin's *Tales of the City*—there's a gay character in there who simply wants 'someone to buy a Christmas tree with'; the moments of intimacy—not especially sex-related—that lift life. Sometimes everything drags, and that can exacerbate any other bad things I'm feeling at any given moment. I think about sharing space, forming a community, getting a lodger... and I always think, well, maybe tomorrow.

Looking back on that now that I've said it, my loneliness isn't merely a social loneliness. It's a physical and a bodily loneliness too, skin hunger—and not in a particularly lustful way either. I want to feel safe and held, to feel the assurance and warmth of a body nearby. I'd like someone to rest my head on their chest, and I similarly have the capacity to rest someone's head on mine. I know it's a cliché but I've got so much love to give and I'm simply wearied by a life with no capacity to give or receive a very intimate love. This isn't a celibacy that I've chosen on a level playing field. Sometimes I hate it. What's the best way to get your head round that?

I struggle even to get my head around what you've just said. Your chosen path of celibacy seems to be unbelievably hard when you put it in such terms—an all-encompassing loneliness which is both social and physical. In fact, all I can compare it to is the unlevel playing field of Christ's own life and journey to the cross. Somewhere, love, including physical intimate love, must be found in Christ. And Christ affirmed our physicality through his incarnation—he showed how much he loved people through being physical and intimate. As a consequence, I believe there must be a meeting place between physical intimate love and celibacy. But I don't know where that could be.

If the ball was in the other court, and I lived in a world where being heterosexual caused me to feel such loneliness, to be in effect a social and physical leper, I wouldn't know how to cope. Even contemplating such a world, I encounter feelings of abandonment and desolation rising up within me. No wonder you sometimes hate it.

Sometimes I'm just sadly resigned, sometimes I'm weighed under with sorrow, sometimes I forget about it for days at a time and get on with life and ministry. But yes, I hate it—for me and for so many others. It's an absolute killer. And for too many people that's horribly and literally true. The prejudice, the fear, the alienation and the self-disgust all make suicide attempts and self-harm too common. It's not a fantastic place to live. But what you said sounds like a useful exercise in empathy. What if heterosexuality was frowned on?

Do you think there's any difference between living alone as a heterosexual single person and as a homosexual single person?

I doubt it. Only in what you're left alone with, what the contents of your head and life actually are. It may be that the chief characteristic of being gay and keeping reasonably quiet about it is a sense of being a stranger in a strange land, not quite speaking the language, not quite knowing the 'correct' or normative responses to things. The Pet Shop Boys use the metaphor in a song, Discoteca, all about trying to get by in a world that's not quite your own, all about the fear of being discovered. I feel a little like that—that one day I'll look too closely at someone on the beach, in the street, react 'wrongly' to something somewhere in the company of people who are watching too carefully...and then the brown stuff will hit the fan—'Is it enough to live in hope that one day we'll be free without this fear? I'm going out and carrying on as normal.' I'm certainly not saying gay Christians should all be in the closet (wherever that might be) but for many Christians discovering they're gay in St Agatha's-by-the-Gasometer in deepest Telford, keeping the hatches down is presently the most obvious answer. Like me, ministering in a big city. Who's waiting outside this mysterious closet? A mob with blazing torches or a welcoming committee? 'Going out and carrying on as normal'—what else is there to do?

Perhaps the degree to which to gay Christians can 'carry on as normal' is equal to the context in which they find themselves. No context is black or white, but for some there will be the darker shade of grey of the mob, and for others the lighter shade of the welcoming committee. I know which shade I'll be praying for.

Incidentally, can we talk about the contents of my head?

Yes, just pour them straight onto the page!

I've talked about the tinnitus, about the background noise of wounding words. But the hardest voice to deal with is my own. There's a huge part of me that finds it difficult to like myself. There's a bad thing going on in my head that surfaces and batters on at me for being gay, for being useless: 'you're just a stupid gayboy,' stuff like that, not always in the second person. It gives me days when I can't bear to look in the mirror, find it hard to meet people's eyes, want to stay in, sometimes can't even bring myself to speak. Now I'm not suggesting I'm 'hearing voices.' I'm sure that a lot—if not all of that—is my conscience, rightly or wrongly reflecting the time and place I grew up, reflecting the company I've kept inside and outside of church, reflecting everything I've heard said about gay people. I'm equally sure that anyone who believes in the devil will identify his hand in exacerbating that, twisting it to accuse me before God. And I'm further sure that it's only the space that you and I and others have hewn out—space for me to be completely myself in—that prevents that pressure, that voice from pushing me back into the kind of depression that I was labouring with seven years ago. As it is, if I'm tired or demoralized or things have being going badly at church, I can take a real pounding off this and be laid low for days.

I'm sure I'm not the only person whose life conspires to fill my head with rubbish and kick what minimal self-esteem I might have in the teeth. At the risk of being blunt, what do you say to that?

Well, I have to say you're not the only person who has this kind of inner warfare going on inside their head. Everyone goes through something similar in terms of working through life's pains and problems. Personally speaking, I don't hear the same 'voices' as you, but nonetheless I have to face up to my own fears and doubts, which at different times are more or less intense. But, having said this, what

you're describing seems to be on another level compared to what I have to face up to in terms of the social and religious pressures.

And then there's falling in love! And by love I don't mean lust, which I'm also subject to, mostly around the checkouts in Tesco or during Hollyoaks. By love I mean that beautiful and awful jelly feeling in my stomach, losing sleep and losing my appetite, drifting off in a conversation because there's one person I can't get out of my head, one person whose kindness and nearness makes me want to laugh and cry and live out loud. That is love, I take it?

Much of what you have described I have certainly felt when I think of my love for my wife...

Well, that happens now and again. And it's a whole love—it's about loving someone for all that they are. It's about as far from a quick and shallow shag as you can get. It's a huge and deep love and I have to live with knowing that great swathes of people close to me wouldn't understand, wouldn't approve. And also with knowing that there's not much point in telling him how fantastic I think he is. It eats my insides away. Sexuality isn't all about sexual intercourse, but anyone who recommends celibacy for gay people needs to understand that they're asking me to sit on my sexuality, a sexuality that is a powerful and an unpredictable thing. They need a good answer when I'm pacing the floor, heart crushed to a pulp, all out of tears and all out of sympathy.

Pass the teapot, will you?

Stay Together

7

Well, the teapot's almost empty, so we'll be wrapping this up shortly! But I think I must reiterate the very basic fact that God is good, and has been and continues to be good to me. And I hope he is to you as well?

Yes. Yes, God is good. I'm still here, so we can confidently assert that his grace is sufficient for my needs. But I'm not about to let this book be wrapped up by the idea that since God's grace is sufficient, we can leave it all to him. It's up to us—all of us—to have that same grace about us. I think that's difficult in the world we have, and difficult in the church we have. There's probably a lot more grace than I think in what keeps being called 'the gay debate,' but there's still a lot that makes me long for more grace for all the hurting people.

I agree. It's also a great shame that the church, the press and the public repeatedly use the term 'the gay debate.' At first glance debate seems an okay word, but the more I think about it, it actually reinforces the different views people have. It may not stop people talking and listening to each other, but it doesn't seem to create a positive and kind atmosphere in which to explore the issues. Dialogue would be a much healthier word—it emphasizes communication and understanding. What do you think about 'dialogue' as opposed to 'debate?'

Well, popularly if not etymologically, debate is too often about two opposing opinions, about making points that build up one and demolish the other. It's adversarial. That may be desirable in a debating chamber or a court of law...but in God's kingdom? In Christ's body? Let's disagree with Mrs Merton, let's not have a heated debate. In my experience, debates rarely build anything or anybody up; rather, they entrench us and our opinions. A whole range of people try to draw Jesus into debate in the gospels and he seems to prefer not to subscribe to it as a useful tool for moving forward. Jesus seems to say very pertinent things, usually from an oblique and unexpected angle. But I'm not Jesus, so I need something else to replace debate, and dialogue is a very good candidate. Dialogue involves a capacity to listen, a capacity to learn, and the possibility of admitting that I may be wrong in matters large or small. Maybe people of opposing views can lend each other a hand to climb out of the trenches and face together a difficulty which hampers our common fight against real evil and our common desire to see Christ proclaimed. I tire of *Channel Four News* showing footage of us waving placards at each other. Let's have some footage of tea and toast. Naïve, I know, but then isn't much of the gospel?